Chinese Military Police Knife, Baton and Weapon Techniques

**Translated By
Chow Hon Huen**

**Edited By
Dennis Rovere**

*BEST WISHES
D Rovere
March '97*

Chinese Military Police: Knife, Baton and Weapon Techniques

ISBN 0-9681346-0-2

Published by:

Rovere Consultants International Inc.
10828 Brae Road, S.W.
Calgary, Alberta, Canada, T2W 1E1

Telephone (403) 253-6032 Fax (403) 252-5980

Disclaimer:

The publisher, author, editor and translator of this manual are not responsible for any injury, or damage of any sort which may result from following the instructions contained herein.

Before embarking on any of the physical activities described in this book, the reader should consult his or her physician regarding their individual suitability for performing such activity.

To our son Anthony. May he never have
the need to protect his life.

Table of Contents

Acknowledgements

In the course of my martial arts training, I was guided by individuals of high moral character and exceptional skill. It is with this thought in mind I make the following acknowledgements:

My teacher Colonel Chang Hsiang Wu. He taught me that "the fight is always the fight of your life."

My teacher Major Chang Yen Ying. She is greatly missed by all who knew her.

My assigned Wu Jing instructor, Mr. Sun Ah-Bill. A great fellow to "hang out" with. His practical experience and skill in modern Chinese military close combat training is a great aid to me in my own teaching.

My host in China, Mr. Ken Tsang. It is only through his diligent efforts I was able to partake in both Wu Jing (Special Military Police) and Gung An (Public Security) close combat training. He was also invaluable in obtaining the training manuals for translation.

Finally, and most importantly, to Chow Hon Huen. Without her support, patience and many hours of painstaking translations, none of this work would ever get into print.

Foreward to the English Translation

Recently, much has been written about the practice of traditional Chinese martial arts and the "performance" art of contemporary Wu Shu. In contrast to this, virtually nothing exists outside China (and little in China) on the close combat use of Chinese martial arts by the military. There are several reasons for this void in the literature:

1.   Secrecy surrounding the "real" practice of martial arts in Mainland China.
2.   Lack of martial artists who understand the application of close combat within the framework of contemporary warfare and low intensity conflict.
3.   Lack of published material from which to draw comparisons between Western and Eastern close combat training.
4.   Lack of information on how Chinese martial arts are adapted for specialized military training.

This manual attempts to change much of the current situation as outlined above. It offers, for the first time in the English language, actual close combat techniques employed by the Chinese Wu Jing (Special Military Police).

Although trained extensively in T'ai Chi, Hsing-I, and Pa-Kua, I was always curious about the realistic application of martial arts to military close combat and security training. In the early 1970s, I received my first taste of this "real life" application through my teachers Colonel Chang Hsiang Wu and Major Chang Yen Ying. This unassuming couple had literally trained hundreds of top instructors and specialized military units for the Chinese army. Additionally, both were combat veterans of the Sino-Japanese (Second World War) and Chinese Civil War. The techniques they passed on to me are ones actually employed in these life-and-death conflicts. In the context of the educational journey I began as a young man in the early 1970s, the 1995 trip to China helped to make my training "complete."

As I stated earlier, the contents of this book are taken directly from several contemporary Chinese military police training manuals. Consequently, the techniques reflect the types of situations peculiar to their specific role in the military and national security of China. From my background I realize, and am quick to point out to the reader, that different techniques (or more drastic applications) may be employed by other branches of their armed forces. (As a qualified expert witness in assault, I also realize many of the techniques, if employed by North American law enforcement, would constitute a liability nightmare!) Nonetheless, these techniques are genuine and are presented as a first time offering to the English reader.

In compiling the text, several compromises in translation were made:

1.   Superfluous text is eliminated. The Chinese language tends to repeat phrases for emphasis. Since this is not a norm in written English, we have, for the sake of clarity and brevity, avoided this practice.

2.   Directions in Chinese are given as "I" and "me" (first person). Since the second person (i.e., "you") and the present tense reads better in English, we have chosen to follow this form throughout.

3.   In some places in the text, we opted for a translation that fits the "mood and flow" of the text rather than a more literal "word-for-word" translation. This is not

to say the text has been altered. Rather, we simply chose to eliminate (or clarify) the ambiguity that a literal translation would present.

One final comment on the techniques. Although the applications presented here are, by and large standard, the knife and baton forms I learned from Mr. Sun in Beijing, are different. (I also learned an empty-hand form not presented in these texts.) We believe, but were not able to verify at the time of printing, that this variation is due to the specialized nature of Mr. Sun's work in the Wu Jing. He functions primarily as a bodyguard and bodyguard instructor for military and government officials. Many of the techniques he demonstrated to (and on!) me, reflect his highly specialized area of expertise.

In future publications we plan to present other aspects of Chinese military close combat including: physical training, improvised weapons, alternate forms and applications (as described above). We also have "in the works" a text on the Chinese Commando version (armed and unarmed applications) of Lien Bu Ch'uan. We hope that you enjoy this book and that it proves to be a valuable aid in your training.

Dennis Rovere and Chow Hon Huen
Calgary, Canada, 1996.

Chapter One

Dagger Attack & Defence Killing Techniques

The dagger is a type of short knife. As a martial arts weapon, it can be utilized for both offence and defence. Besides teaching self-defence, dagger "forms" are also used to keep one fit and healthy.

Dagger "Fitness Form"

This dagger form is divided into two sections of ten movements each. Part One emphasizes forward grip, thrusting/stabbing upwards, and stabbing/thrusting horizontally and diagonally. Part Two emphasizes reverse grip, forward thrust, horizontal slash, and left and right chopping/slashing.

Names of the dagger "Fitness Form's" movement are as follows:

Section One:

Ready Position

1. Upper Block, Thrust.
2. "T" Stance, Withdraw Knife.
3. Step Forward, "Flick" Upwards from Below.
4. Step Back, Withdraw Dagger.
5. Circle Counter-clockwise, Thrust Upwards.
6. Grab, Thrust Diagonally.
7. Bow Stance, Straight Strike.

8. Left Leg Spring Kick.
9. Change Grip, Thrust.
10. Rotate Body, Thrust.

Section Two:

11. "Pressing Step," Left Kick.
12. Turn body, Cut to the Back.
13. Step Forward, Thrust Straight.
14. Shuffle Forward, Slash Right.
15. Press Step, Slash Horizontally
16. Step Back, Execute Lower Block.
17. Hide Dagger, Change Grip.
18. Block, Thrust Upwards.
19. "T" Step, Withdraw Dagger.
20. Step Forward, Thrust.

Conclusion of Form.

Section One:

Ready Position:

Right hand holds the knife. (*Editor's Note—Throughout all techniques, unless stated otherwise, weapons are held in the right hand.*) Arms are down by sides. Make an inner circle (counter-clockwise) movement with the wrist. Palms face the rear. Point of blade is up. Stand straight. Eyes face front. (Figure 1).

Fig. 1

1.   Upper Block, Thrust.

Action:

Left foot steps to the left. As you step, turn body to the left. Bend left arm. Execute a rising block. (Back of the fist faces outward.) Immediately withdraw arm. Place it near the waist. Next, raise right hand and prepare to execute a downward thrust. (Figures 2, 3 and 4).

Key Points:

Right arm raises to head height. As right hand raises, assume a left Bow Stance.

Fig. 2   Fig. 3   Fig. 4

2. "T" Stance (Ding Bu) and Withdraw Knife.

Action: (Continue from previous movement):

Right foot steps up beside left foot. Circle inside with right arm. Stop right hand in front of abdomen. Press left hand against right wrist. (*i.e., Left hand reinforces right wrist*). Bend both knees into a "side squat" position. (Figure 5).

Key Points:

"Suck in" stomach and bend knees. Both legs are together. Point of knife faces to the side. Eyes are on right hand. When forming "T" Stance, right heel does not touch the ground.

Fig. 5

3.   Step Forward, "Flick" Upwards From Below.

Action: (Continue from previous movement)

Take one step forward with right foot. As step is being made, circle arm and immediately flip wrist. Thrust from below to the front. Push left hand to the back left side. (Figure 6).

Key Points:

When thrusting, blade points diagonally upwards. Palm faces outward, "Fist Eye" points down. Assume a Bow Stance. Eyes are on the right foot.

Fig. 6

4. Step Back, Withdraw Dagger.

Action: (Continue from previous movement)

Step backwards with right foot. Draw it close to left foot. Bend knees. As right foot steps, withdraw dagger. Place dagger in front of abdomen. Use left hand to immediately cover right wrist. (Figure 7).

Key Points:

When stepping backwards, assume a "T" (Ding Bu) Stance. Body turns to the right—angling slightly towards the front. Eyes face right/front.

Fig. 7

5. Circle Counter-clockwise, Thrust Upwards.

Action: (Continue from previous movement)

Raise knife and circle from inside to outside. As you circle hand, step forward with right foot. Slash from high to low. (Figure 8).

Key Points:

In "high position," knife should be held at head height. Left hand moves naturally to the back. Point of blade faces upwards. Eyes face right hand. Assume a Bow Stance.

Fig. 8

6. Grab, Thrust Diagonally.

Action: (Continue from previous movement).

Body turns to the left. Left foot steps toward back of the right foot. As step is made, move right hand to the back. Eyes face right/rear direction. (Figure 9). Left hand grabs. Right foot withdraws. Thrust diagonally to the right/front. (Figures 10 and 11).

Key Points:

After left foot crosses and left hand grabs, immediately withdraw right foot. As you thrust, withdraw left hand to waist. Eyes are on the right hand.

Fig. 9   Fig. 10   Fig. 11

7. Bow Stance, Straight Strike.

Action: (Continue from previous movement)

   Body turns to the right. Withdraw right hand to the waist. Left hand makes a fist. Immediately strike to the front. (Figure 12).

Key Points:

   When the strike is made, left arm is straight. "Face" of fist is to the front. "Palm heart" faces down. "Fist eye" points inward. (*i.e., Fist is horizontal*). Eyes face front. Assume a right Bow Stance.

Fig. 12

8.   Left Leg Spring Kick.

Action: (Continue from previous movement)

Withdraw left fist to waist. (Left foot is supported by the right leg). Quickly Spring kick to the front with left foot. (Right [supporting] leg is slightly bent). (Figure 13).

Key Points:

When kicking, body must be straight. Point of dagger faces outside and to the back. Eyes face front. Spring kick is not highter than opponent's groin. Tip of toe is level (straight). Strength reaches point of toe and instep.

Fig. 13

9. Change Grip, Thrust.

Action: (Continue from previous movement)

Land left foot. Turn body to the right and back. Bring right and left foot together. Bend knees. Right hand is on top. With left hand, grasp dagger from below. (Figure 14). Continue turning to the right. Right foot quickly sidesteps to the right. Execute right hand block to the side (back). (Figure 15). Immediately, use left hand to reverse grip. Thrust to the right. (Figure 16).

Key Points:

Dagger is exchanged when body has turned 270 degrees. As left hand thrusts, right hand deflects to the back. Assume a right Bow Stance. Eyes face direction of thrust.

Fig. 14   Fig. 15   Fig. 16

12

10. Rotate Body, Thrust.

Action: (Continue from previous movement)

Immediately turn to the left. As you turn, draw right foot close to left foot. Grasp dagger from below with right hand. Reverse the grip. (Figure 17). Immediately (and quickly), side step to the left. Turn body to the left. Use left arm to block above head. RIGHT HAND NOW HOLDS THE DAGGER. Thrust to the front. (Figure 18).

Key Points:

When thrusting to the front, assume a left Bow Stance. Eyes face left/front direction.

Fig. 17   Fig. 18

Section Two

11. "Press Step," Left Kick.

Action: (Continue from previous movement)

"Press Step" right foot towards left foot. (*Feet are side by side*). Bend both arms. Touch the sides of the body. Eyes face left. (Figure 19). Immediately, kick with left foot. (Toes are pulled back). Body turns to the side. (Figure 20).

Key Points:

Timing for right foot "Press Step" is important. When left foot kicks to the side, body inclines slightly to the right. Eyes face left/front direction. (*i.e., The direction of the kick*).

Fig. 19   Fig. 20

14

12. Turn Body, Cut to the Back.

Action: (Continue from previous movement)

Land left foot in front. Immediately, turn body to back/right direction. Follow with right foot. Slash horizontally to the right. (Figure 21).

Key Points:

Body turns quickly. Centre of gravity is stationary. Left arm bends and covers chest. Eyes face direction of slash.

Fig. 21

13. Step Forward, Thrust Straight.

Action: (Continue from previous movement)

Quickly withdraw right foot (*backwards*). Right and left foot are now side-by-side. Bend both knees. Withdraw dagger to right side of waist. Form a fist with the left hand. (Figure 22). Eyes face right/front direction. Immediately step forward with right foot. Right hand thrusts to the front. (Figure 23).

Key Points:

As you thrust, assume right Bow Stance. Withdraw left fist to waist.

Fig. 22   Fig. 23

14. Shuffle Forward, Slash Right.

Action: (Continue from previous movement)

Shuffle left foot forward in the direction of the right foot. Follow this by stepping forward with right foot. As right foot steps, quickly raise dagger and slash to the left/front direction. (Figures 24 and 25).

Key Points:

Right step and slash must be coordinated.

Fig. 24   Fig. 25

15.   "Press Step," Slash Horizontally.

Action: (Continue from previous movement)

Circle right hand inwards. Immediately after hand circles, shuffle step forward. (Right foot is in front). As you step, slash horizontally from left to right/front direction. (Figures 26 and 27). Point tip of blade down.

Key Points:

As slash travels from left to right, allow left hand to naturally swing to the side. Slash occurs at neck height.

Fig. 26   Fig. 27

16. Step Back, Execute Lower Block.

Action: (Continue from previous movement).

Step backwards with right foot. Turn body to the right. Bring left foot beside right foot. Raise left arm. (Figure 28). Bend both knees. Quickly execute a low block. (Figure 29).

Key Points:

When blocking, bend knees to the side. Use right hand to place dagger on right side of body. Eyes face left.

Fig. 28   Fig. 29

17. Hide Dagger, Change Grip.

Action: (Continue from previous movement)

Bend and block. Touch the leg with back edge of knife. (*i.e. The cutting edge faces outwards*). Quickly reverse grip. (Figure 30).

Key Points:

When reversing grip, hand extends to the back. Palm should also face the back. During this action, thumb, middle finger and index finger, tightly hold "base" of the handle. Immediately change to reverse position. (*i.e., Base of the handle and "fist eye" should both face the same direction*).

Fig. 30

18. Block, Thrust Upwards.

Action: (Continue from previous movement)

Bend left arm. Block to the side. Step forward with left foot. Raise dagger upwards (from the back). Thrusts. (Figures 31 and 32).

Key Points:

As you step forward and block, assume a Bow Stance. When you thrust, point tip of blade down.

Fig. 31   Fig. 32

21

19. "T" Step, Withdraw Dagger.

Action: (Continue from previous movement)

Step up and place right foot next to left foot. As you step, turn body to the left. Withdraw dagger to front of abdomen. (Figure 33).

Key Points:

When body turns to left, right side faces forward. Point of blade faces away from body. Left hand rests on right wrist. Eyes face right/front.

Fig. 33

20. Step Forward, Thrust.

Action: (Continue from previous movement)

Quickly step forward with right foot. Slash from below to front. (Figure 34).

Key Points:

When thrusting, circle arms inward. Tip of blade points to the front. Palm faces back. Left hand should naturally swing to the side and back.

Fig. 34

Conclusion of Form

Action: (Continue from previous movement)

Withdraw right foot internally. (*i.e., Tips of toes hook inward*). Extend both arms out from sides. Circle outwards. Rise. (Figure 35). Next, lower both arms in front of body. Close left foot beside right foot. Settle both hands in front of abdomen. Eyes face front. (Figures 36 and 37). Stand at Attention.

Fig. 35   Fig. 36   Fig. 37

Chapter Two

Dagger Attack and Defence

Attack and defence techniques introduced in this chapter are for situations in which the criminal is attempting to seriously injure or kill the Wu Jing (Military Police) Officer. Techniques in Part One show an officer using a dagger against an opponent armed with a short knife. In Part Two, the officer uses the dagger against a criminal wielding a short club or baton.

Part One

Dagger vs. Short Knife

1.   Capture Arm, Slit Neck.

Situation:

The criminal, using a forward grip, holds the knife in the right hand. (*Editor's Note—As indicated in Chapter One, unless otherwise noted, weapons are always held in the right hand. This is the case for both the officer and the attacker*). He steps forward with right foot and thrusts straight to the chest. (Figure 38).

Defence:

The instant opponent thrusts, turn body to left. Doing so causes thrust to miss. At the same time, grab his wrist with your left hand. Quickly use the right hand to block upwards against the inside of his arm. (This prevents him from withdrawing his right [knife] hand). (Figures 39 and 40). Follow left hand grab with a right hand slash to opponent's neck. (Figure 41).

Hints:

As your body turns left, use right knee to attack opponent's abdomen and ribs. Knee striking, forces opponent to bend his upper body forward. Once in this position, use above technique to restrain him.

Fig. 38

Fig. 39

Fig. 40

Fig. 41

2. Turn Body, Slash.

Situation:

Opponent executes a straight thrust. (Figure 42).

Defence:

As opponent steps forward, quickly turn body to the left. Doing so causes point of his knife to pass by your left side and miss. (Figure 43). Before he can recover (and defend), forcefully thrust knife into his shoulder or chest. (Figure 44).

Hints:

If your body pivots on the spot, lean to the side

when thrusting.

Fig. 42

Fig. 43

Fig. 44

3. Turn Body, Slash Wrist.

Situation:

Criminal steps forward with his right foot. He thrusts to the abdomen or groin. (Figure 45).

Defence:

As thrust is made, step back to escape. Turn your body to the right. This turning action will cause his knife to miss. (Figure 46). Immediately slash downwards on his right wrist. (Figure 47). At the instant the slash is made, step forward with left foot. Once you close distance with opponent, use your right leg to Spring Kick his groin.

Hints:

Withdrawing and slashing the criminal's wrist will cause him to withdraw or drop his knife. If he does this, quickly step forward with right foot and (with your knife), slash his neck.

Fig. 45

Fig. 46

Fig. 47

Fig. 48

4. Shift, Thrust Downward.

Situation:

Criminal thrusts to the upper body. (Figure 49).

Defence:

Shift body to the left. At the same time, use left hand to block opponent's right arm. This action will deflect his knife to the right. It will also make it difficult for him to withdraw his knife. (Figure 50). Quickly take a half-step forward with left foot. Thrust to his abdomen. (Figure 51).

Hints:

When shifting, blocking or stepping forward, be careful that opponent does not step backwards to escape. If he does, he may slash horizontally to the right.

Fig. 49

Fig. 50

Fig. 51

5. Shift, Kick.

Situation:

Prior to the confrontation, the criminal's knife is hidden behind his back. As you close on him, he attempts a downward thrust to the head. (Figure 52).

Fig. 52

Defence:

At the instant of the attack, quickly shift to the back. Immediately, raise left foot. Kick the right side of opponent's chest or right forearm. If applied properly, the descent of the knife can be stopped. Seizing the opportunity, restrain him. (Figure 53).

Hints:

Application of techniques must be performed the instant opponent raises his knife. There can be no hesitation when shifting or kicking. Do not wait until opponent starts downward thrust. OTHERWISE, HE WILL STICK THE KNIFE INTO YOUR LEG.

Fig. 53

6. Shift, Press, Thrust From Above.

Situation:

Opponent thrusts to the head.

Defence:

The instant opponent raises his knife to prepare for a

downward thrust, quickly shift to the left. This will cause
the thrust to miss. (Figure 54). Immediately, use left hand
to deflect and press opponent's right arm. Do not allow
opponent to raise his right hand or slash to the right.
Quickly, stab the criminal in the back of the right shoulder.
(Figures 55 and 56).

Hints:

When shifting, deflecting and pressing to the right,
quickly step forward with the left foot. By getting close to
the opponent, you can prevent him from stepping backwards. You can also prevent him from withdrawing the
right hand to escape.

Fig. 54

Fig. 55

Fig. 56

7.   Deflect, Press, Turn Body, Thrust.

Situation:

Criminal slashes to the head. (Figure 57).

Fig. 57

Defence:

As he begins to thrust, quickly shift body to the left. At the same time, use left hand to deflect outward and push to the right. This redirects opponent's blade to the left—preventing him from attacking or slashing again. (Figures 58 and 59). As you shift and push, withdraw right foot. Immediately turn body away. Position it on opponent's right side. Thrust knife into back of opponent's shoulder. (Figures 60 and 61).

40

Hints:

After deflecting, pressing and pushing, quickly turn to the back. While opponent is totally unprepared, attack and slash.

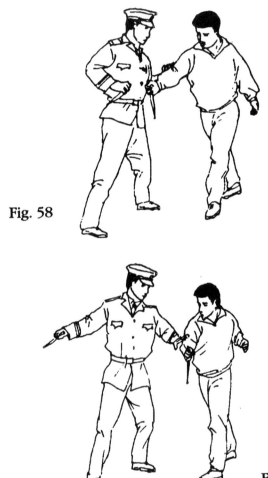

Fig. 58

Fig. 59

Fig. 60

Fig. 61

Part Two

Dagger vs. Baton

1. Block, Strike, Deflect Arm, Thrust.

Situation:

Criminal executes a straight strike with baton.

Defence:

To avoid strike, quickly shift body to left. Raise left hand and deflect outward. At the same time, step forward with left foot to get closer to opponent. This prevents him from using the baton. (Figures 62 and 63). During the actions of shifting, blocking and deflecting, thrust right hand at opponent's stomach. (Figure 64).

Hints:

While shifting, right hand can also bend upward and hook opponent's baton. Left foot quickly steps forward and left fist strikes opponent's right temple. Alternately, left foot side kicks or hooks opponent's front leg to defeat him.

Fig. 62

43

Fig. 63

Fig. 64

2. Defend Against Forward Strike, Shift, Press, Thrust.

Situation:

Opponent uses baton to execute a forward thrust. Separation (distance) between you and criminal is greater than in previous technique. (Figure 65).

Fig. 65

Defence:

Quickly shift to the left to avoid forward thrust. Use this shift to get closer to opponent. Press left hand against his hand or baton. This forces baton to "sink." (Figure 66). Move left foot forward. Thrust right hand at opponent's throat. (Figure 67).

45

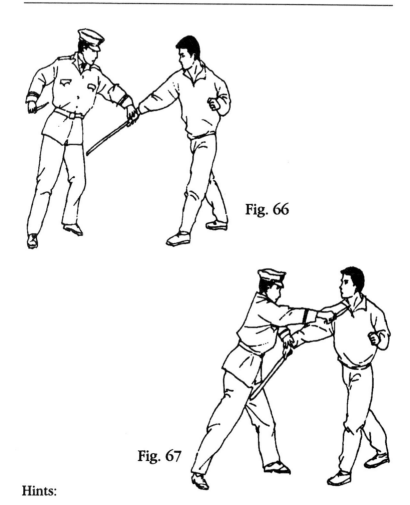

Fig. 66

Fig. 67

Hints:

After shifting body and pressing hand, you must get close to opponent. Failing to do so will allow opponent to easily withdraw baton and step backward. If he is successful, you will lose close contact and the chance for countering his attack.

3. Defend, Strike, Shift, Thrust Downward.

Situation:

Criminal attempts a straight strike to your head or face.

Defence:

"Emergency." (*i.e., Little time to react*). In order to avoid the strike, quickly shift upper body to the right/back direction. (Figure 68). Immediately block and grab opponent's right wrist or baton with your left hand. (Figure 69). If opponent attempts to withdraw his hand, slash his lower abdomen. (Figure 70).

Fig. 68

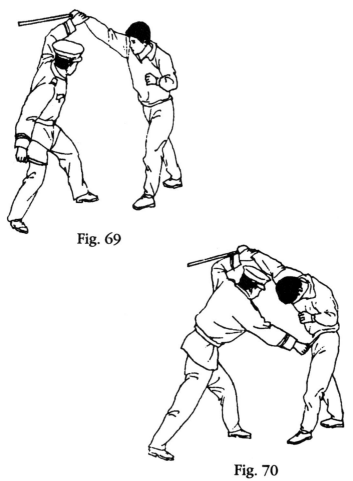

Fig. 69

Fig. 70

Hints:

As you grab, you can also use right foot to "Spring Kick" his groin. Also, if opponent tries to withdraw as you grab his baton, step forward with your right foot to close the distance. As you step, thrust at his abdomen.

4. Bend Upper Body, Shift Left, Slash.

Situation:

Opponent strikes at your head. His blow comes sideways and horizontally from above. (Figures 71 and 72). Defence:

As opponent raises baton, bend upper body forward. Bend both knees so his baton slips past the head. After he misses and before he recovers, shift upper body to the left. Step forward with left foot to close distance. Thrust at opponent's stomach. (Figure 73).

Fig. 71

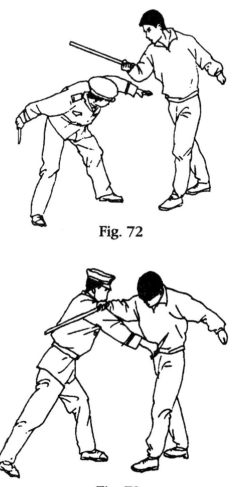

Fig. 72

Fig. 73

Hints:

Immediately after bending forward, continue to drop. Grasp his two legs. Throw him backwards.

5. Shift, Circle Behind, Hook Throat, Thrust.

Situation:

Criminal strikes from above at your head. (Figure 74).

Fig. 74

Defence:

As opponent raises baton, quickly shift body and move to his right side. (Figure 75). Before he withdraws baton, quickly move both feet forward—to his back/right side. At the same time, use your left hand to hook his throat and pull him backwards. Press your blade against his waist or ribs. (Figures 76 and 77). "Then the opponent will not be willing to move." (*i.e. He will be totally restrained.*)

Fig. 75

Fig. 76

Fig. 77

Hints:

During body shift to the right—if you cannot go to opponent's back, use left hand to grab opponent's throat from the front. Use left leg to hook opponent's front leg. Finish by throwing opponent backwards.

Chapter Three

Baton Strikes and Defensive Techniques

The baton (short staff), is of great value for both fitness and self-defence. It is especially important for use by military and security personnel—especially when it is not appropriate to employ firearms.

In order to explain the full use of the baton, the following chapter is divided into two parts: Baton "Exercise Form," and Defensive Techniques (respectively).

Part One
Baton "Exercise Form

Besides being good for physical fitness, baton "exercise forms" also help develop an understanding for application of techniques. This form consists of two sections with a total of twenty movements. Names of each movement in this form are as follows:

Section One:

Ready Position

1. Step Forward, Strike to the Front.
2. Hold Fist, Block Upward.
3. Cross Step, Block Downward.
4. Horse Stance, Block to the Front.
5. Block, Strike Upwards (Above).

6. Bow Stance, Strike with End of Handle.
7. Stamp Foot, Swing Down.
8. Bow Stance, Strike Forward.
9. Resting Step, Vertical Block.
10. Squat, Swing Back.
11. Pivot Step, Flip.
12. Turn Body, Chop.

Section Two:

13. Turn Body, Whip Baton.
14. Press Horizontally to the Lower Front.
15. Block Upwards, Kick to the Front.
16. Squat, Swing to the Front.
17. Raise, Block.
18. Bow Stance, Reverse Thrust to the Front.
19. Turn Around, Block and Strike.
20. Withdraw Baton, Closing Position.

Section One

Ready Position.

Right hand holds baton. (*Editor's Note—As in all other instances, weapon is held in right hand unless otherwise noted*). Palm faces out. Baton touches right side of body. Feet are together. Assume a "ready stance." Eyes face front. (Figure 78).

Fig. 78

1. Step Forward, Strike to the Front.

Action:

Step to the left with your left foot. Bend left arm and block from front to outside. Immediately, strike to lower left direction. (Figures 79, 80 and 81).

Requirements:

When striking, baton should point slightly downward. Eyes face lower front. Form a left Bow Stance.

57

Fig. 79

Fig. 80   Fig. 81

2.   Hold Fist, Block Upwards.

Action: (Continue from previous movement)

Step forward with right foot. Raise baton upwards, above the head. Withdraw left fist to the waist. (Figure 82).

Requirements:

When blocking, right arm is bent. Baton is held horizontally above head. Look to the upper right direction.

Fig. 82

3. Cross Step, Block Downwards.

Action: (Continue from previous movement)

Turn body to left. Immediately cross step by taking one step back with left foot. Block downwards from above. Make a fist with your left hand. Execute a rising block. (Figure 83).

Requirements:

As both legs cross, left heel stays off the ground. Eyes face right rear direction.

Fig. 83

4. Horse Stance, Block Forward.

Action: (Continue from previous movement)

Take one step backwards with right foot. Use right hand to block from outside to front. At the same time, push with front end of left palm. Immediately push both hands forward. (Figure 84).

Requirements:

As left foot steps backwards, body turns left and assumes a Horse Stance. Baton points slightly upwards. It covers the front of the body.

Fig. 84

5. Block, Circle Strike Upwards.

Action: (Continue from previous movement)

Turn body to right. Bend right arm. Circle it inward. Baton is above the head. Follow with left hand. Hold right wrist. (Figure 85). Quickly step forward with left foot. At the same time, swing right hand in an arc to the outside. Flip the wrist and strike horizontally. (Figure 86).

Requirements:

Flipping the wrist, striking, and stepping forward must all be performed sequentially and in rapid succession.

Fig. 85   Fig. 86

6. Bow Stance, Strike with the End of the Handle.

Action: (Continue from previous movement)

Withdraw baton. As you withdraw, use right hand to grab centre of baton. (Both hands are now holding the baton). Immediately strike to the front/right direction with butt end of the baton. (Figure 87).

Requirements:

When preparing to strike, assume a right Bow Stance. Eyes face direction of strike.

Fig. 87

7. Stamp Foot, Swing Down.

Action: (Continue from previous movement)

Shift centre of gravity to the back. Raise right knee. Push baton to the right. Turn body. (Figure 88). Quickly "land" right foot by stamping it on the ground. Right hand swings from below to the outside. (Figure 89).

Requirements:

The push, press, downward swing, and foot stamping must be sequential. When stamping, both legs must be bent. When swinging baton, left hand holds right wrist. Eyes look down.

Fig. 88   Fig. 89

64

8. Bow Stance, Strike Forward.

Action: (Continue from previous movement)

Step forward with left foot. (*i.e. Step to the left/front direction*). Make a fist with the left hand. Bend left arm. Block upwards. As block occurs, right hand strikes forward. (Figure 90).

Requirements:

When striking, assume a left Bow Stance. Eyes face front.

Fig. 90

9. **Resting Stance, Vertical Block.**

Action: (Continue from previous movement)

Turn body to left. Assume a "resting stance." Move right hand to the left. Block vertically in front of the body. (Figure 91).

Requirements:

Left hand is on top. Right hand is below. Both hands push out to the front.

Fig. 91

10. Squat, Swing Back.

Action: (Continue from previous movement)

Step to the right with right foot. Body drops. Swing right hand horizontally from front to lower right. (Figures 92 and 93).

Requirements:

As you swing horizontally, squat. Upper body bends slightly forward. Direction of swing is from front to back.

Fig. 92   Fig. 93

11. Pivot Step, Flip.

Action: (Continue from previous movement)

Quickly stand up. Cross step with left foot and place it in front of right foot. Turn to the right. Raise baton and turn it to the right. Pull it close to the left side of body. Rotate body position. (Figures 94, 95 and 96).

Requirements:

Left hand supports right wrist.

Fig. 94   Fig. 95   Fig. 96

12. Turn Body, Chop.

Action: (Continue from previous movement)

Continue to turn body to the right. Left hand moves naturally to the back. (Figure 97).

Requirements:

When chopping, assume a Horse Stance. Eyes face right.

Fig. 97

Section Two:

13. Turn Body, Whip Baton.

Action: (Continue from previous movement)

Turn body to the left. Deflect to the outside with left hand. Immediately take a large step forward with right foot. Right hand whips baton from below to the front. (Figures 98 and 99).

Requirements:

When whipping baton, turn to the side. After deflecting, left hand moves to the back. Eyes face right.

Fig. 98   Fig. 99

14. Press Horizontally to the Lower Front.

Action: (Continue from previous movement)

Rotate right wrist (and baton) inward. Immediately withdraw the tip of the right foot inward. Turn body slightly to the left. Press baton horizontally in front of the right (front) side. (Figure 100).

Requirements:

While rotating wrist and pressing horizontally, assume a half-horse stance. Left hand blocks in front of the chest. Eyes face right.

Fig. 100

15. Block Upwards, Kick to the Front.

Action: (Continue from previous movement)

Step left foot towards right foot. As this occurs, hold baton with both hands and block upwards. Quickly kick to the front with the right foot. (Figure 101).

Requirements:

Block moves from the front to above the head. As you kick with the right foot, hook your toes. Strength is distributed through the whole foot.

Fig. 101

16. Squat, Swing to the Front.

Action: (Continue from previous movement)

After the kick, land right foot and drop body. Swing right hand horizontally from the outside to the lower front. Move left hand naturally to the back. (Figure 102).

Requirements:

Side squat. (*i.e. Lean slightly to the side when swinging baton*). Upper body leans forward.

Fig. 102

17. Raise, Block.

Action: (Continue from previous movement)

Withdraw right arm, bend it, circle it inwards, and to the outside. Hold right wrist with left hand. Baton blocks to the upper right direction. (Figure 103).

Requirements:

After swinging horizontally, raise baton and point tip of baton to the front. Eyes face right.

Fig. 103

18. Bow Stance, Reverse Strike to Front.

Action: (Continue from previous movement)

Withdraw baton. Quickly move both feet forward. Point handle of baton forward. Use left hand to grasp middle of baton. Push forward. (Figure 104).

Requirements:

As you step forward, flip baton so that ends exchange position. Assume a right Bow Stance when striking.

Fig. 104

19. Turn Body, Block, Strike.

Action: (Continue from previous movement)

Turn body to the left. Make a fist with left hand. Block upwards. Strike forward with baton. (Figures 105 and 106).

Requirements:

As the left arm blocks, body turns to the left but stays on the same spot. When striking forward, assume a left Bow Stance. Eyes face front.

Fig. 105   Fig. 106

20. Withdraw Baton, Closing Position.

Action: (Continue from previous movement)

Grab baton with left hand. Flip it under right armpit. (Withdraw baton to right side of body). (Figure 107).

Requirements:

Both hands grab baton using the "tiger mouth" grip.

Fig. 107

Closing Position:

As baton is withdrawn, left foot moves close to right foot. Right hand holds baton against right side of body. In Standing (at attention) Position, eyes face front. (Figure 108).

Fig. 108

Part Two
Baton Strikes and Defence

Techniques with the baton are primarily designed for defence and counterattack against the long staff and dagger. Emphasis is placed on first defending, and immediately following up with a strike. (*As opposed to beginning the techniques with a pre-emptive strike*).

Section One
Baton vs. Long Staff

1. Side Block, Straight Strike to Head.

Situation:

Criminal holds a long staff. He attempts a horizontal strike to the left. (Strike is approximately waist height). (Figure 109).

Defence:
As opponent begins strike, hold both ends of baton. Turn upper body to the left. Block staff along left side of the body. (Figure 110). Once block is complete, push baton forward. Step forward with right foot, closing the distance with the opponent. Grasp baton with right hand. Turn wrist and strike opponent's head. (Figure 111).

Hints:

As opponent strikes, try to close distance with him.

79

This will control his long range attack and restrict the force of the staff during the strike.

Fig. 109

Fig. 110

Fig. 111

2.   Block, Deflect, Chop.

Situation:

Criminal attempts to strike the head from the upper right direction. (Figure 112).

Defence:

As the strike begins, step forward with the left foot. (Alternately, step back with the right foot). Grasp both ends of the baton. Block above the head. (Figure 113). Quickly turn body to the right. Deflect staff and press to the right. As you press, hold opponents's staff in front of the chest and stomach. This prevents him from withdrawing the staff. (Figure 114). Grasp baton with LEFT HAND. Turn wrist and strike opponent's head. (Figure 115).

81

Fig. 112

Fig. 113

Fig. 114

Fig. 115

Hints:

When pressing, pay attention that the opponent doesn't turn the staff around and strike from below.

83

3. Block, Deflect, Thrust to Chest.

Situation:

Opponent strikes to head using same method as described above. (Figure 116).

Fig. 116

Defence:

Hold baton with both hands. Block upward. Immediately push, deflect, and turn body to the left. (Figures 117 and 118). Step forward with right foot to close distance with opponent. As this occurs, use back end of baton to poke opponent's chest or throat. (Figure 119).

84

Fig. 117

Fig. 118

Fig. 119

Hints:

During blocking or deflection, the opponent may step backwards. If this occurs, grasp baton with right hand and strike his head.

4.   Block, Turn to the Left.

Situation:

Opponent holds staff with both hands. He steps forward with the left foot and thrusts at your chest. (Figure 120).

Fig. 120

Defence:

As the staff comes forward, side step to the right. (Right foot steps and body follows. This takes the body out of the line of attack). Grasp both ends of the baton and attack from the front side downwards. (Figures 121 and 122). Next, close the distance with the opponent by moving both feet forward. Strike sideways to the opponent's neck. (Figure 123).

Hints:

Turning the body, blocking, and striking downwards must all be performed in quick succession. Do not give the opponent any opportunity to escape.

Fig. 121

Fig. 122

Fig. 123

5. Shift, Grab, Strike Forward.

Situation:

Opponent uses thrusting method as described in the preceding.

Defence:

Quickly shift body to the left to evade opponent's strike. Grab staff with left hand and press down. Strike opponent's face with baton. (Figures 124 and 125).

Fig. 124

Fig. 125

Hints:

While shifting and grabbing, the opponent's staff can also be pulled to the right. If this occurs, use left foot to kick opponent's groin.

90

6. Shift, Block, Chop to the Right.

Situation:

Criminal holds staff with both hands. He attempts a straight thrust. (Figure 126).

Fig. 126

Defence:

As thrust is initiated, shift body to the left. Use baton to block the staff to the right. (Figure 127). Step forward with left foot to close distance with opponent. Grasp baton with both hands. Strike opponent on left side of his neck. (Figure 128).

Fig. 127

Fig. 128

Hints:

Shifting, blocking, pressing downwards, stepping to close distance, and striking sideways, all have to be coordinated and executed in quick succession.

7.   Block Downwards, Strike.

Situation:

In reality, criminals will sometimes use the long staff to strike or thrust at the feet. (Figure 129).

Fig. 129

Defence:

In this type of situation, either withdraw or shift both feet to the side. Use right hand (which holds baton) to deflect staff from the front to the outside. (Figure 130). Move right foot forward to close distance with opponent. Flip (or snap) the baton and chop opponent's head. (Figure 131).

93

Fig. 130

Fig. 131

Hints:

During blocking and deflecting, you can also use the baton to roll along the staff and chop the criminal's left hand.

8. Trap Staff, Strike Groin.

Situation:

Opponent steps forward and attempts either a strike or direct thrust to the waist. (Figure 132).

Fig. 132

Defence:

(This technique is used regardless of whether the strike is sideways or straight). If there is no time to step backwards, quickly turn sideways. Use the left arm to trap the staff, and forcefully put it forward, (Figure 133). The opponent will either attempt to pull the staff back or raise his right foot to kick. At the moment this occurs, use the baton to snap (forcefully) to his groin. (Figure 134).

Fig. 133

Fig. 134

Hints:

When fighting against a long staff, pay particular
attention when stepping forwards and backwards. Do not
allow yourself to be hit by the end (point) of the staff.
Generally speaking, if you are hit by the centre of the staff,
you will not be injured so easily.

Section Two
Baton vs. Dagger

(Editor's Note—As with all previous sections, unless indicated otherwise, knife and baton are both held in the right hand.)

1. Block Wrist, Shift, Chop.

Situation:

Criminal attempts a sudden thrust at your abdomen. (Figure 135).

Fig. 135

Defence:

Immediately "suck in" the stomach and move backwards. Before the opponent can withdraw the blade, use baton to strike downwards on his right arm. This will either cause his arm to drop, or the knife to fall from his hand. (Figures 136 and 137). Side step to the left (with the left foot). (This allows you to maintain a certain fighting distance). Immediately after stepping, flip the wrist and use baton to chop criminal's neck. (Figure 138).

Fig. 136

Fig. 137

Fig. 138

Hints:

After blocking the wrist and stepping backwards, use the right foot to kick the opponent's groin.

2. Strike, "Hang," Side Kick.

Situation:

Criminal steps forward and thrusts to either the face or the chest. (Figure 139).

Fig. 139

Defence:

As soon as the thrust is initiated, step backwards. Using baton, snap/strike the opponent's wrist from the front to upper left direction. This will cause the opponent's arm to rise. (Figure 140). As opponent's attention shifts to his arm, reposition right foot and side kick his chest or abdomen. (Figure 141).

100

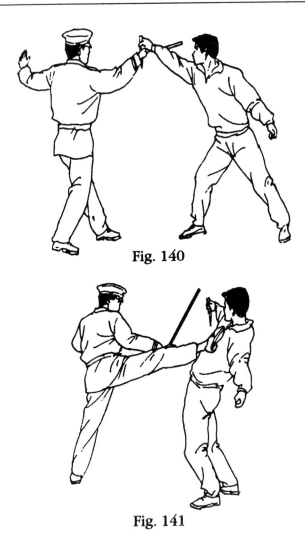

Fig. 140

Fig. 141

Hints:

At the same time you shift backwards, turn to the left. The body should angle as you snap/strike his waist.

3.   Side Shift, Strike Downwards.

Situation:

During an altercation, the criminal attempts a straight thrust at your abdomen. (Figure 142).

Fig. 142

Defence:

Shift to the back/right to avoid (escape) the thrust. (Figure 142). While shifting, use baton to thrust at opponent's lower abdomen. (Figure 143).

102

Fig. 143

Hints:

After thrusting, withdraw baton to prevent it from being grabbed by the opponent.

4.   Shift, Block, Chop to the Right.

Situation:

Criminal thrusts at your chest. (Figure 144).

Defence:

Shift body to the left. This allows the opponent's knife to pass by the right side. (Figure 145). Immediately grasp baton with both hands and strike opponent's right arm. Follow up with a sideways chop to his neck. (Figures 146 and 147).

Fig. 144

Fig. 145

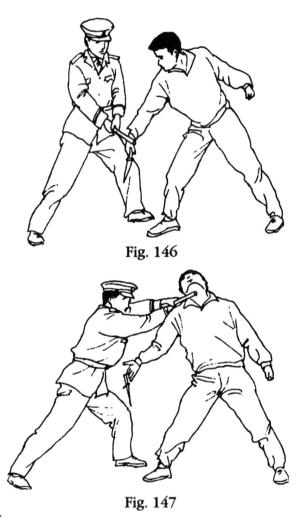

Fig. 146

Fig. 147

Hints:

Timing is most important in coordinating the actions. Before chopping, you must position yourself beside the opponent.

5.   Shift, Big Step, Chop to the Outside.

Situation:

Opponent executes a straight thrust. You quickly shift back. He withdraws knife, steps forward, and thrusts again. (Figures 148 and 149).

Fig. 148

Fig. 149

Defence:

As opponent attempts second thrust, shift to the left side. Make a big step to the outside with the left foot to avoid the second attack. Immediately strike opponent on right side of his neck or head. (Figure 150).

Fig. 150

Hints:

After avoiding the first attack (and before he can withdraw his knife for a second attack), you can also use your right leg to side-kick opponent's stomach or ribs. To avoid this, opponent must "withdraw his abdomen." As his upper body leans forward, use end of baton to (forcefully) poke at the back of opponent's right shoulder.

107

6. Deflect Knife, Turn Body, Chop.

Situation:

Criminal steps forward and executes a straight thrust.

Fig. 151

Defence:

Withdraw backwards. Using baton, block his right wrist. (Figures 151 and 152). Right foot steps backwards. Swing baton and deflect to the outside. (Figure 153). When opponent misses and sees you stepping away, he will attack again. In response, move body to the outside right position. Use baton to strike sideways at his neck. (Figures 154 and 155).

Fig. 152

Fig. 153

Fig. 154

Fig. 155

Hints:

Step backwards and strike at the same time.

110

7. Lean Forward, Strike Waist.

Situation:

Opponent slashes at the head. (Figure 156).

Fig. 156

Defence:

As he slashes, lean your body forward. Bend both knees ("half-squat" position) so the knife passes above your head. (Figure 157). Move body to the left so that you are quite close to opponent's right side. Step forward with left foot. Grasp baton with both hands and strike sideways to opponent's abdomen or ribs. (Figures 158 and 159).

111

Fig. 157

Fig. 158

Fig. 159

Hints:

As you lean forward, or when you squat and move to the left, use this time to strike opponent's legs with the baton.

8.   Block Upwards, Kick.

Situation:

Opponent uses knife to strike downward at your head. (Figure 160).

113

Fig. 160

Defence:

In this situation, either step forward with left foot, or step backwards with right foot. Grasp both ends of baton and quickly block upwards. (Figure 161). Follow this with a right (foot) kick to his abdomen. (Figure 162). Alternatively, use your leg to "spring-kick" opponent's groin. (Figure 163).

Fig. 161

Fig. 162

Fig. 163

Hints:

Should the opponent withdraw backwards during either the kick or "spring-kick," land right foot and grasp baton in right hand. Strike the opponent's head from the outside.

9.   Block, Strike the Head.

Situation:

Criminal stands with left foot forward. He stabs at your head. (Figure 164).

116

Fig. 164

Defence:

Hold baton in right hand. Block knife. At the same time, shift body back. (Figure 165). As you block, opponent side kicks with right foot. (Figure 166). Withdraw left foot backwards. At the same time, use baton to block his front leg (travelling from above, downwards). Either opponent's right foot must land or be withdrawn backwards. The instant either occurs, flip your wrist and "snap-strike" his head with the baton. (Figures 167 and 168).

117

Fig. 165

Fig. 166

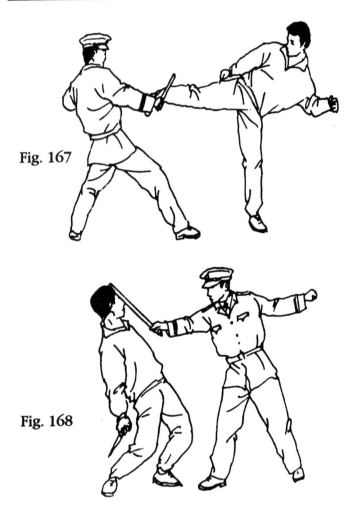

Fig. 167

Fig. 168

Hints:

When striking the head, opponent may raise his arm to block upwards. If this occurs, quickly withdraw baton and execute a straight thrust to his chest or abdomen.

10.   Block Upwards, Sweep Downwards.

Situation:

You are quite close to the opponent. Suddenly, he steps forward with the right foot and uses his knife to attack from above. (Figure 169).

Fig. 169

Defence:

Immediately withdraw. Use baton to block upwards. This prevents knife from continuing downwards. (Figure 170). While blocking, step backwards with left foot. Immediately use baton to strike opponent's right leg from the outside. (Figure 171).

Fig. 170

Fig. 171

Hints:

When blocking or striking downwards, you can also flip the wrist and strike opponent on the right side of the neck.

121

11. Block, Side Kick.

Situation:

Criminal steps forward with left foot and executes a straight thrust. (Figure 172).

Fig. 172

Defence:

Quickly withdraw both feet backwards. Your upper body follows and leans/shifts slightly back. Using baton, block opponent's right arm. (Baton's motion should travel from front to left, thereby deflecting knife to the right). (Figure 173). Follow your block with a right side kick to his chest or abdomen. (Figure 174). Alternatively, execute a "spring-kick" to his groin.

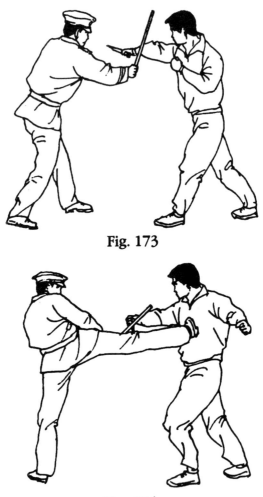

Fig. 173

Fig. 174

Hints:

During the process of blocking opponent's thrust, you could also allow baton to follow the inside of his arm. Strike his face or head.

Chapter Four

(Empty Hand) Weapon Disarms

Techniques introduced in this chapter emphasize empty hand disarms of handguns and knives.

Part One

Pistol Disarming Techniques

(Editor's Note—As in all sections, unless otherwise noted, weapons are held in the right hand).

1.   Shift, Grab, Block, Knee Strike, Disarm.

Situation:

Criminal points pistol at your chest. He orders you to raise your hands. Using his left hand, he begins to search your upper body. (Figures 175, 176 and 177).

Fig. 175

Fig. 176

Fig. 177

Defence:

      i.   Immediately twist body to right. This causes you to move out of alignment with the barrel of the pistol. Use your left hand to quickly grab opponent's right hand and the back part of pistol. Push forward to deflect pistol to the right (and away from your chest). (Figures 178 and 179).

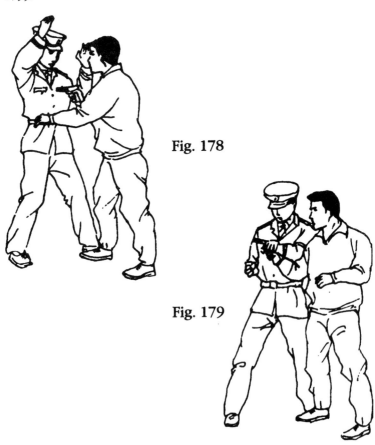

Fig. 178

Fig. 179

ii.   Flip your right hand and grab opponent's wrist from below. Turn body to the left. At the same time, twist pistol so it points to opponent. Use right knee to strike his groin. Block his wrist and disarm him. (Figures 180, 181 and 182).

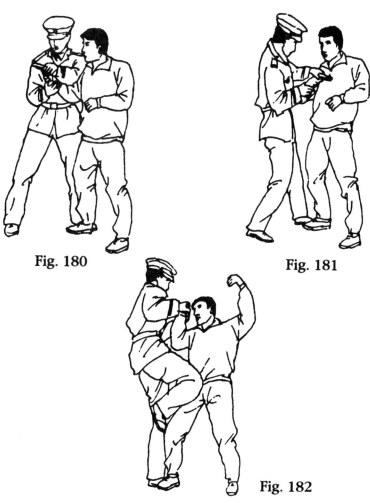

Fig. 180

Fig. 181

Fig. 182

iii.   When the criminal begins to search your upper body, you may shift to the outside and use your left hand to grab opponent's right wrist. Right hand then quickly grabs back of his hand and front part of pistol. Aim pistol back towards opponent. (Figures 183, 184, 185 and 186). In order to restrain opponent, use a knee strike to his groin.

Fig. 183

Fig. 184

Fig. 185

Fig. 186

2.   Shift, Grab, Push Upward, Kick, Disarm.

Situation:

Criminal points pistol at your head. Using his left hand, he begins to search your upper body. (Figures 187 and 188).

130

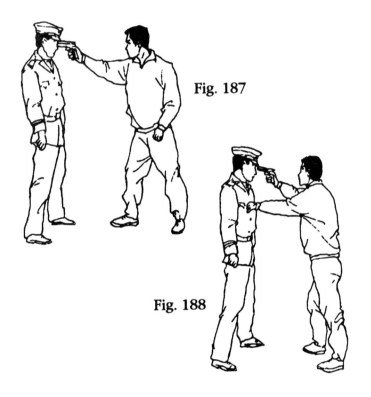

Fig. 187

Fig. 188

Defence:

      i.   Immediately shift to the right to avoid line of fire. Quickly use right hand to grab inner side of opponent's wrist. This deflects pistol to the right. (Figures 189 and 190).

      ii.   Use left hand to grab pistol from below. Push upwards. Twist his wrist so that pistol points upwards. (Figures 191 and 192).

      iii.   Next, force his hand to the outside. Execute a groin kick with your right foot. (Figure 193).

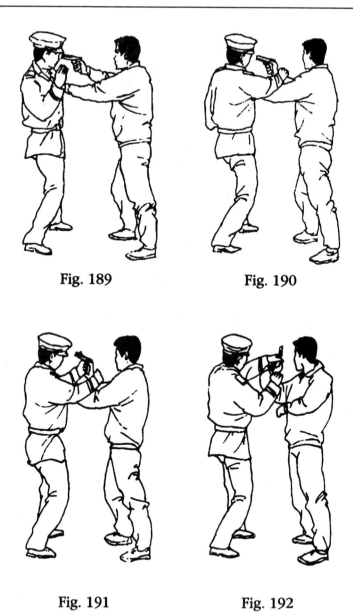

Fig. 189

Fig. 190

Fig. 191

Fig. 192

Fig. 193

3.   Grab, Hold, Poke, Knee Strike, Disarm.

Situation:

Criminal points pistol at your chest. He begins to search your upper body. (Figure 194).

Defence:

i.   Shift to outside to avoid line of fire. (Figure 195).

ii.   Move left arm from below. Rotate it, grab, and pull pistol to the left side of your body. (Figures 196, 197, 198 and 199).

iii.   Poke his neck with your right hand. To restrain him, use a right knee strike to his groin or abdomen. (Figures 200 and 201).

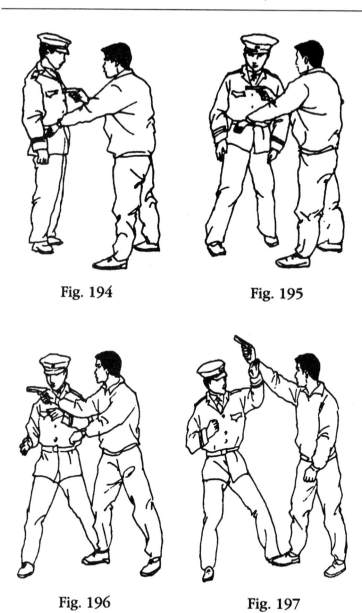

Fig. 194   Fig. 195

Fig. 196   Fig. 197

Fig. 198

Fig. 199

Fig. 200

Fig. 201

4. Shift, Block, Lock Arm, Disarm.

Situation:

Criminal points pistol at your back. (Figure 202).

Fig. 202

Defence:

 i. Quickly turn to the left and shift upper body out of line of fire. At the same time, use left arm to block to the back. Strike inner side of opponent's hand to deflect pistol. (Figure 203).
 ii. Step forward with left foot to close distance with opponent. Using your right hand, grab his groin. This causes opponent to draw his groin and abdomen back and shift his attention (focus). (Figures 204 and 205).

iii.   Push your left arm to the outside. Bend it and use it to hold opponent's right arm. With your right hand, grab his right shoulder and upper arm. Turn body to the right. This forces opponent's right arm back—locking it. (Figures 206, 207, 208 and 209). After arms are locked, free your right hand and disarm criminal. (Figures 210, 211 and 212).

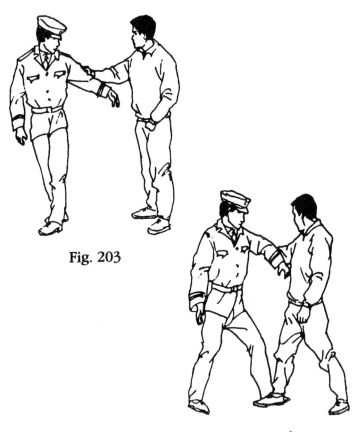

Fig. 203

Fig. 204

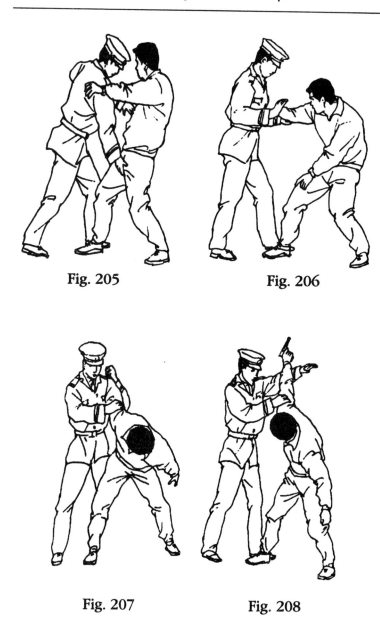

Fig. 205

Fig. 206

Fig. 207

Fig. 208

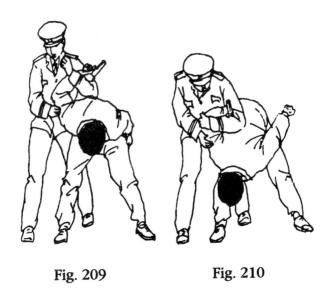

Fig. 209 Fig. 210

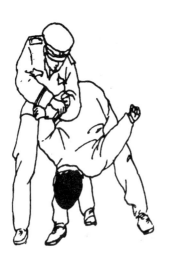

Fig. 211 Fig. 212

5. Block Backwards, Lock Throat, Disarm.

Situation:

Criminal points pistol at your back. He uses left hand to search your pants (i.e., lower body). (Figures 213 and 214).

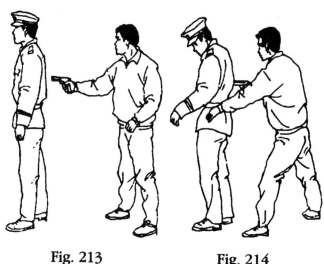

Fig. 213   Fig. 214

Defence:

i.   Quickly turn to the right. Use right arm to lock opponent's arm. Force arm to outside so that pistol is deflected. (Figure 215).

ii.   As you turn body, step forward with left foot. (You will end up on right side of opponent.) Immediately bend right forearm to hold criminal's right forearm. (Figures 216 and 217).

140

iii.   Grasp criminal's throat with left arm. Pull to the back to restrain him. (Figures 218 and 219).

Fig. 215   **Fig. 216**

Fig. 217   **Fig. 218**

Fig. 219

6. Lock, Strike, Disarm.

Situation:

Criminal points pistol at your back. He uses his left hand to search your body. (Figure 220).

Defence:

Pivot body to right. (i.e. Turn but remain on the same spot). Swing right arm back to deflect pistol. (Figure 221). Immediately bend arm to lock opponent's right arm. Step forward with left foot to close distance with opponent. Use left fist to strike his temple from the side. This blow will knock him out, thereby allowing him to be restrained. (Figures 222 and 223).

142

Fig. 220   Fig. 221

Fig. 222   Fig. 223

Part Two

Empty Hand vs. Knife

(Defensive techniques in Part Two are divided into two sections. Section One defences are all against a downward strike from above. Defences in Section Two, are against a straight thrust).

When defending against a criminal who uses a knife, it is important to understand two key points:

1.   Only move if the opponent moves. When the opponent begins to move (i.e., has committed to executing the technique), you must move faster than he does.
    e.g.: When an opponent strikes downward at your head, quickly move forward to get closer to the opponent. As the knife is being raised (but hasn't begun to move downward), use grabs and blocks to restrain the opponent. Prevent knife from striking downwards and follow up with the most simple and direct "close body methods" or chin-na to disarm him.
2.   If the attack is too forceful or aggressive, avoid contact.
    When the criminal strikes, pay attention to his coordination of shifting and attacking. Timing and execution of all steps in proper succession are most important. When the opponent strikes and misses, he has "expended all his energy." His body is not protected. Before he recovers to make the second movement, use kicks, strikes, grabs, throws, etc., to restrain him.

Section One

Techniques Against a Downward Strike

1.   Hold elbow, Grab, Disarm.

Situation:

Criminal holds knife in right hand. He steps forward and strikes downwards at your head. (Figures 224 and 225).

Fig. 224   Fig. 225

145

Defence:

i.   The moment opponent raises his knife, shift your head to the outside. Extend your left hand. Step forward with left foot to close distance. Block and grab opponent's right wrist. (Figure 226).

ii.   Right hand grabs his elbow and pushes upward. Right foot steps forward and hooks his front leg. (Figures 227 and 228).

iii.   As you push opponent's arm back, use left hand to forcefully pull downwards. Right hand pushes elbow. These opposing forces will throw the criminal to the ground. After he lands, use your right knee to restrain him. (Figures 229 and 230).

Fig. 226   **Fig. 227**

Fig. 228

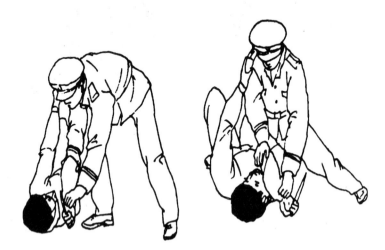

Fig. 229   **Fig. 230**

2. Bend Elbow, Reverse Lock, Disarm.

Situation:

Criminal strikes downward at your head.

Defence:

i. Immediately shift to the outside. Use left arm to block and grab opponent's wrist. (Figures 231 and 232).

Fig. 231   Fig. 232

ii. Quickly slide right hand underneath opponent's arm. Grab his right forearm. Step forward with right foot and hook his right leg. (Figure 233).

148

Fig. 233

iii.   Use left hand to twist and press wrist. Bend right arm and hold criminal's upper arm. This position locks the opponent's elbow and forces it backwards. His body will also be forced to extend and bend backwards, completely controlling his movement. (Figures 234 and 235).

Fig. 234

Fig. 235

3. Roll Wrist, Press Arm, Disarm.

Situation:

Criminal uses a cleaver or similar weapon to strike your head. (Figure 236).

Fig. 236

Defence:

  i.   Immediately shift body to outside. This causes the strike to miss. (Figures 237 and 238).
  ii. Use left hand to grab opponent's right forearm. Turn body to the right. Raise your left elbow. Press his arm and rotate it to the outside. This causes opponent's hand (and cleaver) to rotate inward and his palm to flip to the outside. (Figures 239 and 240).

150

iii.   As you rotate and press against his arm, use right hand to grab the back of his hand. Disarm him. (Figures 241, 242, 243 and 244).

Fig. 237   Fig. 238

Fig. 239   Fig. 240

Fig. 241   **Fig. 242**

Fig. 243

Fig. 244

4.   Squat, Shift, Reverse Sweep, Restrain.

Situation:

Criminal holds a cleaver. He uses it to strike either sideways or directly downward to your head. (Figures 245 and 246).

Defence:

Immediately lean forward and drop. This action will cause the cleaver to miss. Quickly turn to the right and use right leg to reverse sweep opponent. This technique will cause him to fall backwards. (Figures 247, 248, 249, 250, 251 and 252). Disarm him.

Fig. 245

Fig. 246

Fig. 247

Fig. 248

Fig. 249

Fig. 250

Fig. 251

Fig. 252

5.   Shift, Grasp the Groin, Disarm.

Situation:

Criminal holds a cleaver and strikes at your head. (Figure 253).

Fig. 253

Defence:
i.   Immediately shift to the outside. Move outside opponent and use right hand to grab his arm. (Figures 254 and 255).
ii.   Use left hand to grab his groin from behind. Pull upwards, dropping him forward. He will now be under control. (Figures 256 and 257).

Fig. 254   Fig. 255

Fig. 256

Fig. 257

Section Two

Techniques Against a Straight Thrust

1.   Lock Wrist, Restrain, Throw, Disarm.

Situation:

Criminal holds knife and thrusts at your chest. (Figure 258).

Fig. 258

Defence:

i.   Shift to the left. Use left hand to grab the outside of his wrist. (Figures 259 and 260).

ii.   Quickly use right hand to push and grab back of opponent's right hand. Fold his wrist so that knife points to his chest. Use force to push knife and stab him. (Figures 261 and 262).

If criminal attempts to fight back, or you cannot fold his wrist inward, quickly change direction of the force. Press outward. Step forward with right foot and hook his right leg from the back. Turn body to the left and throw opponent onto the ground. Press right knee on opponent's chest to restrain him. (Figures 263, 264, 265 and 266).

161

Fig. 259　　　　　　Fig. 260

Fig. 261　　　　　　Fig. 262

Fig. 263   Fig. 264

Fig. 265   Fig. 266

2.   Dislocate Arm, Disarm.

Situation:

Criminal thrusts at your abdomen or ribs. (Figure 267).

Fig. 267

Defence:

i.   Quickly step backwards. Block with left hand and grab upper side of ciminal's wrist. (Figure 268).
ii.   Push arm to outside. At the same time, use right fist to hook punch upwards into the abdomen. This forces him to withdraw abdomen and shift his attention. (Figures 269 and 270).
iii.   As he withdraws abdomen, use right arm to hook his elbow and push it upwards. Force opponent's elbow to bend backwards. (Figures 271 and 272). Push

164

and turn body to the right. Right hand presses and left hand pushes forward with force. This action will easily dislocate opponent's elbow. (Figures 273, 274 and 275).

Fig. 268

Fig. 269

Fig. 270

Fig. 271

Fig. 272

Fig. 273   **Fig. 274**   **Fig. 275**

167

3. Shift, Hook Block, Poke Neck, Disarm.

Situation:

Criminal thrusts at your abdomen or chest. (Figures 276 and 277).

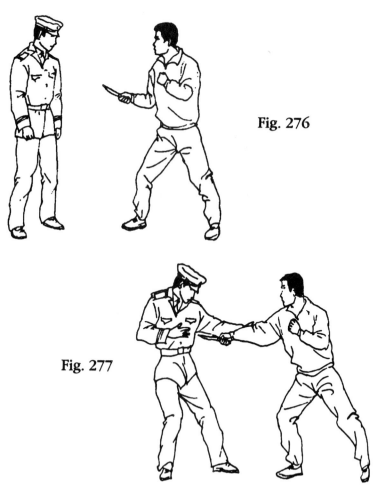

Fig. 276

Fig. 277

Defence:

    i.   Quickly shift outward. Body faces sideways. Use left hand to hook block and grab opponent's right forearm. (Figures 278, 279, 280, 281 and 282).

    ii.   Poke neck with right hand. Use your right knee to strike his groin. (Figures 283 and 284). He will lose the strength to fight.

Fig. 278

Fig. 279

Fig. 280

Fig. 281

Fig. 282

Fig. 283

Fig. 284

4.   Hook, Throw, Lock Arm, Disarm.

Situation:

Criminal thrusts at your abdomen or ribs. (Fig. 285).

Fig. 285

Defence:

   i.   Shift body to outside to avoid thrust. Use right hand to grab opponent's right wrist from the side. (Figures 286 and 287).

   ii.   Turn body to right. Step forward with left leg to hook opponent's front leg. Use left hand to push from the outside and grab the back of his elbow. Grabbing, hooking and pushing, will cause the opponent to be thrown to the ground. (Figures 288, 289 and 290).

   iii.   Place left foot on opponent's right shoulder.

Use both hands to hold his arm and twist it backwards, (i.e., immediately place his arm behind his back). Push opponent's right forearm with your left leg. This will prevent him from fighting back. (Figures 291, 292 and 293).

Fig. 286

Fig. 287

174

Fig. 288

Fig. 289

Fig. 290

Fig. 291

Fig. 292

Fig. 293

5. Carry, Throw, Stamp, Disarm.

Situation:

Criminal thrusts at your abdomen. (Figure 294).

Fig. 294

Defence:

i. Quickly shift body to right. This places you on the inside of the opponent. Use left hand to grab opponent's right wrist. (Figure 295).

ii. Next, land right foot between opponent's two legs. Follow with your right arm and either grab his groin or hold his leg. As you grasp, raise your chest, push with the legs, and lift the opponent. (Figures 296, 297 and 298).

iii. Throw the opponent to your left side. (Figures 299 and 300).

iv.   Grab his arm with both your hands and rotate outward. Quickly stamp on his face with your left foot. (Figures 301 and 302).

Fig. 295

Fig. 296   **Fig. 297**

179

Fig. 298

Fig. 299

Fig. 300

Fig. 301

Fig. 302

6. Shift, Grab, Lift Elbow, Disarm.

Situation:

Criminal thrusts at your chest. (Figure 303).

Fig. 303

Defence:

      i.   Shift body to outside. Use right hand to grab opponent's wrist from the side. Twist it to the outside. (Figure 304).

      ii.   Turn body to right. Step forward with left foot and land in front of the opponent's two feet. (Alternately, withdraw your right foot). Quickly use your left shoulder to carry opponent's right forearm. (Figures 305 and 306). At the same time, grab his arm with both hands and force-fully pull his left shoulder. Both forces acting in opposition can easily dislocate or injure opponent's elbow. (Figures 307 and 308).

Fig. 304

Fig. 305

Fig. 306

Fig. 307

Fig. 308

7.   Lock, Fold Elbow, Disarm.

Situation:

Criminal thrusts at your head and neck. (Figures 309 and 310).

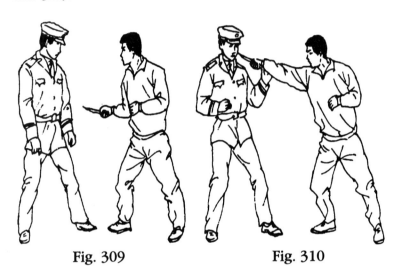

Fig. 309   Fig. 310

Defence:

i.   Quickly shift to the outside. At the same time, use left hand to block and grab outside of opponent's elbow. (Figure 311).

ii.   Bend right arm and push opponent's right forearm from below towards the front. (Figure 312).

iii.   Use left hand to grab elbow and pull downward. As you are doing this, push with right arm. Quickly step forward with right foot and hook opponent's right leg from the back. Immediately move your left hand through

185

the front and grab your own right forearm. Lift with left arm and press elbow. (Figures 313, 314 and 315). This action will securely lock opponent's right arm.

Fig. 311

Fig. 312

Fig. 313

Fig. 314

Fig. 315

Appendices

Appendix A

As published in the January 1996 issue of "Inside Kung Fu" magazine.

Wu Jing

Close-Combat Techniques

Wu Jing military martial arts concentrate on training and executing completely practical and often lethal techniques against single and multiple armed and unarmed opponents.

By Dennis Rovere

(In March 1995, I travelled to Mainland China to undergo training with close-combat instructors in the Chinese military and Gung An Bu [Public Security Administration]. My trip marks the first time anyone outside the ranks of the Chinese military or Special Police Units has been afforded such a privilege. It is only through the concerted efforts of Ken Tsang of Housley's Alberta Inc., that I was able to overcome the political and diplomatic hurdles to

receive this training. For his invaluable help, I am truly grateful).

Considered by many to be the "lethal weapons" of the Chinese military, the Wu Jing (Military Police) Special Close Combat Training Unite, or as they were always referred to, the Special Force, are martial arts experts, par excellence. (I sometimes found the terminology and military ranking system confusing. Although in China, Wu Jing literally translates as military police, it does not have the same connotation as in English. They are not a conventional police unit, bur rather a [military] national security service. The group I am now associated with is referred to as the Special Force because they are responsible for training military units both within and outside the Wu Jing).

From this elite corps in Beijing came my assigned instructor, Sun So-Bin. Sun is currently one of the top close-combat experts in Mainland China today. Not only does he instruct the military, but he also serves as well as trains bodyguards to several high-ranking military and government officials. During my training and interviewing, Ah-Bill (as he preferred to be called), spent a great deal of time explaining, comparing techniques, and giving (often painful) demonstrations. I wasn't the only one to be on the receiving end of Ah-Bill's demonstrations—even Ken (who is not a martial artist, and was present only to translate), unwittingly ended up a "pupil." Ken's "introduction" to the world of close combat occurred during our first meeting with Ah-Bill.

Ah-Bill was in the practice area anxiously awaiting the arrival of his new student—me. Although we had not met, he had been told to expect a Canadian who was both well-trained in military close combat, and traditional

190

Chinese martial arts. While I was busy getting myself in order, Ken went on ahead and entered the practice area first. Ah-Bill, seeing an obvious civilian (civilians do not train with the military), and expecting a foreign Chinese, immediately began to "try Ken out."

Shortly after, I entered the area, only to be greeted with cries of, "I'm the translator, he's the martial artist!" After apologies, many good laughs (and Ken complaining for a week about being kicked and bruised), we carried on with the business at hand.

Can You Fight?

Testing and demonstration is regular in this type of training. Throughout my time in China, neither the military or Gung An instructors ever asked what "rank" I held in martial arts. Instead they would constantly ask me to explain, or "freefight" (often with weapons) or approach subjects indirectly to gauge the quality of my previous training and teaching ability. Since I was Canadian, they fully expected me to be versed in more sport-oriented forms of combat such as boxing, wrestling, judo, etc.—all of which are quite different than military close combat. After it was made known to them who my teachers are, they fully understood why my techniques and teaching philosophy so closely resembled theirs.

My martial arts training had been under Col. Chang Hsiang Wu and Major Chang Yen Fan Ying. In the 1930s, Col. Chang was the chief instructor of close combat and military strategy at the Central Military Academy of China at Nanjing. His responsibilities included the training of officer/instructors at the Academy.

A tai chi, hsing-I and paqua master, Col. Chang had

studied under such notable teachers as Li-li Jou, Sun Lu
T'ang, and the Yang family.

Major Chang Yen Fan Ying is a senior student of the
famous martial artist and national hero, Du Shen Wu. She
was chief instructor of close combat to the Chinese Commandos and Chinese Women's Militia at Changsa and
Baoding.

As Ah-Bill explained, hands-on demonstrations and
"field testing" are necessary so that one can understand the
differences in the application of similar techniques; and one
can understand the overall effectiveness of the Chinese
army's form of close combat.

Deadly Killing Art

What I witnessed and experienced is not the "flashy"
wushu we are accustomed to seeing from the Mainland.
Here, instead, is a deadly killing art completely stripped of
all performance or competitive aspects. Their military arts
concentrates on training and executing completely practical
and often lethal techniques against single and multiple-
armed and unarmed opponents.

To become an instructor in the Wu Jing, a candidate
must complete four years of intensive training and a minimum of one year practical field experience. The pace is
gruelling with all members of the unit spending an average
of six hours per day in a multi-component training pro-
gram.

One of Ah-Bill's favourite training components is
sandbag training, designed to toughen specific areas of the
body and develop the ability to strike with speed and
power. Maximizing injury to the opponent and minimizing
damage to the soldier, is the name of the game. Some of

the areas conditioned include elbows (three specific spots), knees, toes (the front toe kick to the pubic bone is a particular close combat "favourite"), shins, etc.

I was surprised to discover that certain strikes common in Western military hand-to-hand fighting, are not utilized by the Wu Jing. For example, the Chinese train and use extensively both the punch and hammerfist strike. They do not however, use either the backfist or knifehand.

Ah-Bill explained that there are several reasons for avoiding the use of such techniques. First, open-hand strikes such as the knifehand, expose the bones of the hand to injury. This is especially true in a fast-paced, close combat setting where (even among well-trained individuals), exact positioning and precise striking angles are sometimes difficult to attain. Chinese close combat techniques may employ the use of pressure point grabs and restraints (chin-na) etc. To facilitate grasping, the bones of the hand must be kept free from injury.

Secondly, locking techniques are more easily applied when the hand is in the open position. A closed fist makes the wrist stronger and less susceptible to joint manipulations and twisting. Thirdly, Ah-Bill believed that more force can be delivered using the fist in closed position. Having felt his strikes, I tend to agree.

Not to the Groin

Another technique not encouraged or trained is groin kicking. Ah-Bill notes that this kick is avoided for two main reasons: it is considered unethical, as it may cause severe permanent damage; and most people anticipate such an attack and train to defend against it.

I found this statement regarding ethics confusing.

When asked to elaborate, Ah-Bill gave the following explanation:

"Even though we are trained to kill, that is not necessarily our primary function. We are concerned with controlling and diffusing a situation efficiently and quickly with a minimum of injury. We try to use enough force as is necessary—lethal force is the last resort in lethal situations ... While a killing technique can be necessary on the battlefield, it may not be the most appropriate method to use against civilians. Strikes such as the groin kick can cause too much damage. If our force is excessive and uncontrolled, then we are not performing our duties properly."

(Another instructor volunteered a more traditional explanation. Damage to the groin may prevent reproduction and therefore end a man's lineage. In Chinese society, not to have descendants is considered very serious. Therefore, in more ancient times, this unethical form of attack was avoided except in the most serious of situations).

Forms practice only plays a part in the initial stages of training. Recruits are taught several basic forms specially designed for military use. Each form concentrates on specific aspects of close combat and encompasses (respectively) the use of such things as empty hand, knife (offence and defence), and baton. Forms are strictly practical in application and contain no superfluous movements such as salutes or fancy jumping kicks.

A simple example of this is an empty-hand form I learned. It consists of punches, knee and elbow strikes, takedowns, dislocates, and finishing techniques such as chokes or strangles. (Finishing techniques are employed mainly after the opponent has been taken to the ground). Training in the practical application of these forms does not occur in the comfort of the gymnasium, but rather in such places as muddy, rain-drenched fields, and even on the hood of a Jeep! (Remember, the Chinese army always trains to deal with a superior enemy in as realistic an environment as possible).

Standard Weapons Training

Since the Wu Jing is a Special Military Police Group, members undergo extensive training in the use of standard weapons such as the baton. Their training in this area differs somewhat from Western military police units I have had the opportunity to observe or train. For example, the baton is often coupled with hand strikes and even low kicks. Although the Wu Jing officer is armed, he still believes in utilizing every part of the body to his advantage.

Knife forms and knifefighting are not primarily taught to the Wu Jing as an offensive means of combat (although that is a realistic option). Rather, this training is used as a means of fully understanding the ability of an armed and highly trained opponent at close quarters. In this real world of close combat, nothing is left to speculation. The Chinese army is not interested in academic or theoretical approaches to weapons defence—only the real may apply (and be applied). My observation on the number and severity of scars instructors have received (both in training and in real-life encounters) reinforces this need for life-saving techniques and no-nonsense full-contact training. (It should be noted that Ah-Bill's group is also quite well versed in the area of sentry removal and takedowns, as well as the close combat use of improvised weapons).

To deal effectively with high levels of threat in crowds or large gatherings, this Special Force is thoroughly

195

versed in fighting against multiple unarmed and armed opponents. Ah-Bill's group is not, however, delegated the task of SWAT team. This is the primary function of another branch of the Wu Jing. (Members of this branch are capable of such feats as climbing the outside of a five-story building (barehanded), using the drain pipe as a ladder. They are also proficient in both orthodox and unorthodox SWAT tactics).

Although proficient in the use of firearms, Bo Biu (bodyguards) try to avoid employing their weapons or using any obvious display of force in public. In China, very few civilians possess or have access to firearms. As a result, the bodyguard's high degree of skill is usually more than adequate to handle most threats without resorting to a "shootout."

Another limitation in the use of firearms is the "crowd factor." It would be too easy at a diplomatic function or public gathering to have bystanders (or important dignitaries) caught and killed in a crossfire. This is especially true if escalation of the situation occurred from using a pistol as the first line of defence.

Told this, I naturally assumed the Wu Jing would have developed sophisticated methods of handcuffing criminals. Ah-Bill laughed when I expressed this thought. He explained that after criminals are taken to the ground in these situations, handcuffs are usually not needed. In cases where uncooperative criminals have to be held, the Wu Jing officer simply draws his weapon at this time and holds them against the wall or on the ground until backup arrives. Although I know that in reality the Wu Jing are adept at improvising restraints using belts, rope ties and the like, I fully understand the point Ah-Bill is trying to make. The most serious threats are handled by the most serious men—the Chinese Military "Special Force."

Appendix B

Article published in the June 1996 issue
of "Inside Kung Fu" magazine.

Wu Jing
Knife Combat
Techniques

Realistic, practical, and deadly, are only a few
of the words that accurately describe the Wu Jing's
brand of knife combat.

By Dennis Rovere

In the Chinese Wu Jing (Special Military Police), knife
techniques are not primarily taught for offensive use in
combat. To these specialists, offence is secondary. Of
much greater value is the notion that knife combat is a
means of fully understanding the reality of close quarter
conflict against an armed and highly skilled enemy. Training against the blade impresses upon (and teaches) soldiers
realistic, life-saving defensive techniques for survival in

actual combat.

Knives (or daggers) are just one implement in the repertoire of weapons utilized by the Wu Jing. Soldiers also train with and master baton and firearms (more conventional pieces of police apparatus), empty hand striking/ fighting techniques, and improvised weapons. Not only are these weapons used for self-defence, but each one (including the knife) can be employed in arrest and restraint procedures.

(It should be noted that a single edged blade, regardless of length, is always referred to as a knife. The dagger on the other hand, may be single or double edged, and is always relatively short in length).

Last Resort

According to Wu Jing instructors I trained with, unless you are in combat in the field, killing is viewed as a last resort. This is why certain methods are often emphasized over more lethal "solutions." Baton, belt, unarmed, and some improvised weapons, are all considered self-protection "tools." A knife, on the other hand, is strictly classified as a killing weapon. Even when a dagger is employed as a "restraint mechanism," the likelihood of inflicting serious damage is almost always a certainty. This philosophy of killing as a last resort, is the reason military bodyguards (Bo Biu) prefer not to draw their weapons unless the suspect is armed, dangerous, and is preparing to draw (or has drawn) his weapon. By employing "extreme response only in extreme circumstances," the bodyguard lessens the chance of having bystanders or persons in their care, injured or killed.

Although the instructors' team trains an average of

six hours per day when not on assignment, they do very little forms practice. A typical breakdown in training schedule for the instructors is as follows:

- 1 hour running/jogging.
- 3 hours weight training and calisthenics.
- 1 hour sandbag training.
- 1 hour full-contact free fighting (with gloves).

(Free fighting may include defence against an armed opponent or multiple attack/defence training. It may also include weapon disarms and retention techniques).

Because they are a military unit, the Wu Jing concentrates more on crippling/disabling the opponent through striking, than employing restraints as a primary means of control.. This is especially true in knife defence techniques where the disarm is usually preceded by a strike intended to break or paralyse specific target areas on the body. (I encountered the opposite choice in technique when I trained with the Gung An [Public Security]. Of all the techniques I learned and saw demonstrated by the Gung An, the majority involved the use of Chin Na for arrest and control).

No Place For Forms

Forms practice is relegated almost exclusively to recruit training or presented for demonstration in the form of group exercises. (As you may recall from my previous article, the Special Military Police Instructors are discouraged from training in martial arts prior to coming into the unit. This "restriction" prevents an instructor candidate from learning flashy or impractical techniques from performance oriented Wu Shu. Since most recruits will have little or no previous martial arts training, initiation into practical combat through forms practice becomes a logical place to begin).

So, unlike the instructors, an ordinary recruit spends (at least initially) a fair amount of time in forms training. Not only is there long "kata-like sequences" to memorize, but recruits can also look forward to the shorter, more explosive, physically demanding (and repetitive!), sequences of combinations of strikes, blocks, counters, throws, and group choreographed training exercises. All exercises, whether performed solo or against other recruits, are executed in perfect unison in true military fashion.

Group exercises are often quite brutal. Training occurs during all types of weather conditions with both men and women kicking, striking, and throwing each other with full force. I have seen female recruits engage in free-sparring and multiple attack/defence training against their male counterparts. This entire exercise was conducted in ankle-deep mud and pouring rain!

Training For All Occasions

As with all military forms, different sections of the knife form train and emphasize different aspects of strategy and technique. For example, the first section of one form I learned emphasizes such things as the reverse grip, multiple thrusts, and slashing techniques using both the blade and the point of the knife. Another section of this same form concentrates on the forward grip, anti-Chin Na techniques that trap the opponent's hand with the knife blade, straight thrusts, and "takedowns with finishes." Since this is military close combat, some of the movements also teach soldiers how to use the knife to kill enemy sentries or soldiers in full battle gear.

The primary purpose of this initial training is to familiarize the soldier with movements and combinations that he/she may use against another armed combatant. (Or that can be used against them). Presenting the basics of movement and characteristics of the dagger in such a manner allows for the development of an effective (unarmed) strategy of knife defence. Remember, the Wu Jing is only interested in proven, effective methods of combat. Theory and conjecture, while interesting, is best left in the classroom, and not carried onto the battlefield. These techniques therefore, represent basic, efficient (i.e., employable in high-stress situations) means of handling the weapon.

Once basics are learned through the forms, the recruit next progresses to the application stage of training. To fully understand all the training components in this stage, I have chosen for the sake of clarity and brevity, to present these sections using my own categories.

First begin by breaking knife combat down into two basic situations:

- The soldier is armed with the knife; and,
- the soldier is unarmed (i.e., does not have or is not using the knife).

Strategy in both situations comprises both offensive and defensive techniques.

In situations where the soldier is armed with a knife, the techniques include (but are not limited to): offensive tactics against an unarmed opponent (including anti-Chin Na methods), knife vs. knife (offensive and defensive), and combat against an armed opponent. This latter category includes sentry removal and arrest and control of an armed assailant. Typical examples of weapons carried by an armed assailant are the baton, melon knife, cleaver, hatchet, and shovel. Although several of these are bladed weapons, their method of employment (hacking, swinging) differs from that of the knife—hence the different category of training.

Weapon Retention

In situations where the soldier is unarmed (i.e., empty hand), training covers unarmed defence against a knife-wielding opponent, several knife (or bladed weapon) wielding opponents, or a combination of armed and unarmed opponents. Weapon retention techniques such as retaining your assault rifle or sidearm on guard duty, while the opponent attacks with a knife, are also trained. Use of the baton to defend against the knife is relegated to the baton section of training. However, even here, the basic strategies of knife combat are applied.

One of the principles of weapons' training in the Wu Jing is "the weapon never acts alone." Simply stated, the movement of the weapon is coupled with one or more "empty hand" techniques. These are used to enhance the knife attack, and may come either before or after the knife technique. Such movements may distract the opponent, prepare the way for a thrust or slash, or follow the knife blow to keep the opponent physically or mentally off-balance. Implementation of this whole body approach to combat is initiated, reinforced and developed in forms training. Side kicks, Chin Na techniques, knee, elbow and hand strikes, are all integrated and used with simple slashing and thrusting techniques.

One simple example of such integration is a strike/slash combination to the face. In this instance, the attacker slaps the right side of the opponent's face immediately before he slashes the left side of the neck. Not only does slapping momentarily disorient the opponent but the force also turns the head to the left, thereby aiding the slashing action.

Gripping the knife usually occurs in one of two ways:

- Reverse grip, with the blade facing the forearm; and,
- hammer fist grip, with the point of the blade forward.

In both instances, the majority of the cuts are accomplished with the front one-third of the blade and the point.

If, while in a reverse grip position, a slashing motion is attempted, the point of the knife both leads the movement and initiates contact with the target. Thus, technique-wise, there is no instance where a cutting surface does not directly face the opponent. (The obvious advantage to this approach is that one technique allows both single or double-edged weapons to be utilized with equal efficiency).

When the dagger is held in the reverse grip, the blade faces to the inside. This allows the blade to be employed in anti-Chin Na techniques (such as "circular counters" to an opponent's attempt at grabbing the weapon arm or wrist). This orientation also properly aligns the cutting edge for reverse upward thrusts designed to penetrate under a military flak vest.

Stances and stepping are natural. That is, there are no exaggerations in the depth of the stances or length of the step for the sake of "drama" or reach. In real life encounters, such large motions would prove dangerous to the Wu Jing officer—especially on muddy, icy, or wet terrain. Cross stepping and complete (i.e., 360 degree) turning actions of the body, are kept to a minimum. In fact, I only observed two instances where these types of body motions occurred.

The first instance is a sequence called the "Fork Step with Multiple Thrusts." If grappled, the defender cross steps to close on the inside of the opponent. This step is coupled with the previously mentioned reverse upward thrust through the groin area. The follow up is "Turn Body and Thrust Downward—a 360 degree body turn in which the opponent is grabbed and pulled forward with the left hand. While the opponent falls forward, or is attempting to straighten his body to regain balance, the knife is thrust into the neck with the right hand. The angle is such that penetration occurs in the region between the helmet and the collar of the vest.

The second instance occurs in an elbow strike and slash combination. The attacker cross steps to the inside of his opponent and elbow strikes him in the chest. As the opponent's head thrusts forward, the attacker executes a double slash to this target.

Realistic, practical and deadly, are only a few of the words that accurately describe the Wu Jing's brand of knife combat. It is through this understanding and application of strategy in training, that helps make the Special Military Police of China one of the world's foremost exponents of close combat.

Appendix C

Offensive Use of

the Dagger

The dagger is a standard issue military weapon. Its offensive use (i.e., attacking) involves specialized combat training. A "weapon of choice" of Special Forces and other "elite personnel," daggers are often employed in situations where firearms are either not available or unsuitable for use.

This section serves as an introduction to the offensive use of the dagger and the points that are vulnerable to its attack.

(*As with all other examples in this book, these also assume the dagger is held in the right hand.*)

1. Holding the Dagger

i. Normal (Reverse) Grip:

Fist eye points upward. Palm faces to the left. Point of the dagger extends in alignment to the "fist wheel." (Figure A-1).

Fig. A-1

ii. Forward Grip:

Fist eye faces upward. Palm faces left. Point of the dagger extends downward from fist eye. (Figure A-2). (*Editor's Note—In both grips, the hand position does not change. Only the orientation of the blade is altered.*)

Fig. A-2

2.   Offensive Methods Employing the Reverse Grip

i.   Right Diagonal Thrust to the Neck

Grip dagger in your right hand. Raise right arm. Thrust at left side of opponent's neck. (Angle of travel is from upper right to lower left.) (Figure A-3).

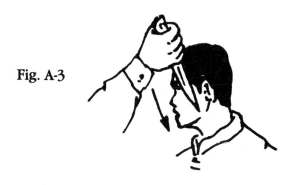

Fig. A-3

ii.   Left Diagonal Thrust to the Neck

Raise dagger towards your left shoulder. Thrust/stab downwards into right side of opponent's neck. (Angle of travel is from your upper left to lower right). (Figure A-4).

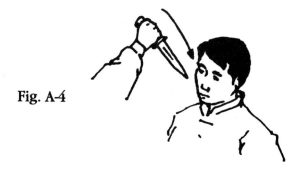

Fig. A-4

iii.   Right Side Thrust to Left Side of Ribs

Stand slightly to the right of criminal. Use your left hand to grab his right shoulder. Thrust dagger from right to left, piercing opponent's left side. (Figure A-5).

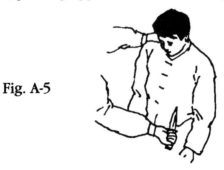

Fig. A-5

iv.   Right Side Thrust to Stomach

A right side thrust is mainly used as a continuous attacking technique.

Begin by executing a left diagonal slash to opponent's head. If opponent steps backwards to dodge attack, step to the left with your right foot. Thrust to the right into his stomach/right side. (Figure A-6).

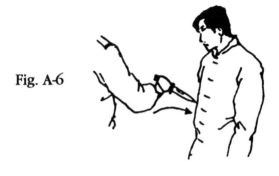

Fig. A-6

v.   Upward Thrust to Stomach

An upward thrust is mainly used as a continuous attacking technique.

Attempt a thrust/slash at opponent's neck. If he steps backwards to evade, quickly step forward with your right foot. Execute an upward thrust into his stomach. (Figure A-7).

Fig. A-7

vi.   Control from Behind Using the Reverse Grip

You are standing behind the criminal. Use your left hand to grab his left shoulder. Pass dagger past his left shoulder. Tightly press blade against opponent's throat and neck. (Figure A-8).

Fig. A-8

3. Offensive Methods Employing the Forward Grip

i. Straight Thrust to Throat:

Using the forward grip, grasp dagger in your right hand. Place it directly in front of your chest/abdomen. Thrust at opponent's throat. (Figure A-9).

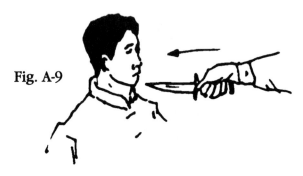

Fig. A-9

ii. Slash Throat:

Extend right arm towards your left shoulder. Moving from left to right, slash opponent's throat. (Figure A-10).

Fig. A-10

You can also slash or chop right side of opponent's neck. (Figure A-11).

Fig. A-11

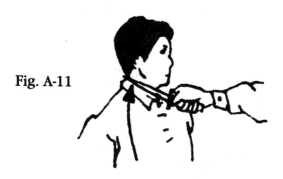

iii.   Vertical Chop/Slash from Above:

Raise right arm. Slash or chop vertically downwards at opponent's face. (Figure A-12).

Fig. A-12

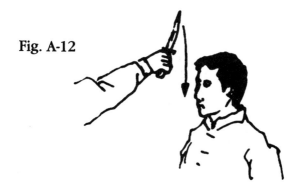

iv.   Vertical Slash from Below:

Extend right arm downward. Thrust (vertically) upwards into opponent's stomach or chest. (Figure A-13).

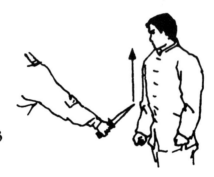

Fig. A-13

v.   Stab Right Side:

Extend right arm downward. Thrust upward into opponent's left side. (Figure A-14).

Fig. A-14

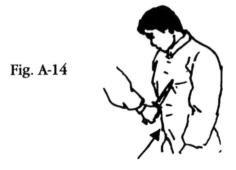

vi.   Thrust at Abdomen:

Extend right arm downward. Use dagger to thrust upwards into opponent's stomach. (Figure A-15).

Fig. A-15

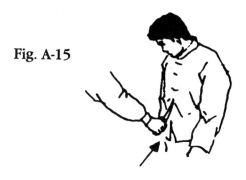

vii.   Stab at Legs:

You are standing behind opponent. Thrust downward and use dagger to stab or slash his legs. (Figure A-16).

Fig. A-16

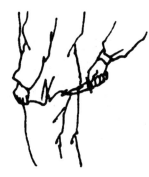

viii.　Choke and Press Blade Upward:

You are standing behind opponent. Extend your left arm across his left shoulder. Lock opponent's throat. Using the dagger, press/stab his right side. (Blade should be held approximately waist height to the opponent.) (Figure A-17).

Fig. A-17

ix.　Use Dagger to Restrain from Behind:

You are standing behind opponent. Use your left hand to grab opponent's left shoulder. Extend right hand (and dagger) around opponent's right shoulder. Press blade of dagger against his throat. (Figure A-18).

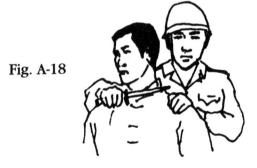

Fig. A-18

x. Block with Dagger and Chop:

During combat, opponent kicks at your stomach with his right foot. Use blade of dagger to block and chop opponent's right calve. (Motion of blade is from inside, outward). (Figure A-19).

Opponent may strike at you with his right fist. If so, use dagger to block and chop his right forearm. (Figure A-20).

Fig. A-19

Fig. A-20

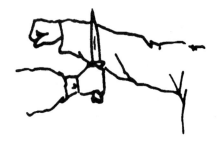

Appendix D

Offensive Use of the Baton

The baton is considered a non-lethal weapon. It is widely used in both law enforcement/security and the military police. During combat against criminals (lit. rioters) it can be used to administer an electric shock.

(Editor's Note: Unless on special duty, uniformed officers of the Chinese Wu Jing (military police) and Gung An (public security) rarely carry firearms. To assist in crowd control/anti-riot work and close combat against minimally armed opponents, officers often carry a special riot baton. This baton is of standard length but differs from the regular baton in two ways:

1.   It has a rubberized (insulated) covering.

2.   It has two small protrusions at one end. Contained inside this baton is a cattle prod-type device. The protrusions are touched against the criminal's skin delivering an electric shock. One such shock usually removes the criminal's "will to fight.")

The baton can also be used to chop, thrust, block, restrain, and press block. For practical purposes, you must consider the situation and whether or not the criminal's actions warrant its use. Never use the baton to blindly chop and strike. Always have a clear target.

Requirements for effective offensive use are speed, precision and strength. This chapter discusses the basic methods of attack and defence/counters with the baton.

1. Chop to the Head:

Opening position: Using a forward grip, hold the baton in your right hand. Ready yourself for combat against the opponent.

Attack Position: Raise the baton. (Figure A-21). Chop straight downward to the (front) top of opponent's head. (Figure A-22).

Fig. A-21

Fig. A-22

2. Thrust to the Face:

Place baton in front of your chest. When opportunity arises, execute a straight thrust to opponent's face. (Figure A-23).

Fig. A-23

3. Right Diagonal Strike to Neck:

Raise baton diagonally to the right. Immediately strike left side of opponent's neck. (Figure A-24).

Fig. A-24

4. Left Diagonal Strike to Neck:

Raise baton diagonally to left. Immediately strike the right side of opponent's neck. (Figure A-25).

Fig. A-25

5. Thrust to Abdomen:

Drop right arm so that baton and arm form a 90 degree angle. Thrust at opponent's abdomen. (Figure A-26).

Fig. A-26

6.   Snap Upwards at Groin:

Drop point of baton.   Quickly snap upwards at opponnent's groin.   (Figure A-27).

Fig. A-27

7.   Use "Base" of Baton to Poke Stomach:

Step forward with right foot.   Turn body to left. Lower baton so handle faces right.   Use end of baton's handle to poke opponent's stomach.   (Figure A-28).

Fig. A-28

221

8. Block to the Outside:

Opponent attempts to stab you in the chest.

Immediately step to the right with your right foot. Turn body to the left. Use baton to block opponent's wrist. (Blocking motion is from outside to inside). (Figure A-29). Use a "Left Diagonal Strike to Neck" technique to counter-attack.

Fig. A-29

9. Block to Inside:

Criminal attempts to stab you in chest or face.

Immediately step forward and to the left. Turn your body to the right. Use baton to block opponent's wrist. (Blocking motion is from inside to outside). (Figure A-30). Use a "Right Diagonal Strike to Neck" techinque to counter-attack.

Fig. A-30

10. Step Backwards and Block:

Criminal thrusts dagger at your groin.

Immediately withdraw. (i.e., Step backwards.) Use baton to block and press opponent's right wrist. (Motion is from inside to outside.) (Figure A-31). Immediately begin counterattacking.

Fig. A-31

11. Block Upwards with Baton:

Criminal thrusts dagger at your head or shoulders.
Using both hands, grasp baton at each end. Block
attacker's right wrist with middle part of baton. (Figure A-
32). Follow block with a groin kick.

Fig. A-32

12. Intercept and Press with Baton:

Criminal attacks your legs and groin.
Immediately withdraw. Using both hands, grasp
baton at each end. Press criminal's right wrist with middle
of baton. (Figure A-33).
If criminal attempts a groin kick, use the same
method to press his foot. (Figure A-34).
Release left hand hold on end of baton. Attack
opponent's head.

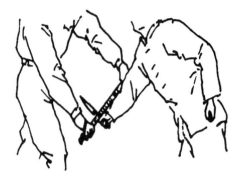

Fig. A-33

Fig. A-34

13. Block Leg and Strike Head:

Criminal uses his right leg to attempt a side kick to your knee.

Immediately step backwards. Use baton to block opponent's right foot. (Motion travels from inside to outside.) (Figure A-35). Attack criminal's head. (Figure A-36).

Fig. A-35

Fig. A-36

14. Block Leg and Strike Neck:

Criminal attempts a right side kick to your ribs (left side).

Immediately step forward and to the right. Turn body to left. Push baton to left with both hands. (Middle part of baton blocks opponent's right foot.) (Figure A-37).

Release left hand. Execute a left diagonal strike to right side of opponent's neck. (Figure A-38).

Fig. A-37

Fig. A-38

Dennis Rovere

In 1974, Dennis Rovere became the only non-oriental to receive instructor's certification in martial arts from Colonel Chang Hsiang Wu (Chinese Army, retired). Colonel Chang is the former chief instructor of military strategy and close combat at the Central Military Academy of China at Nanjing. An expert in Hsing-I Ch'uan, he was responsible for training large numbers of officers and instructors prior to and during the Second World War.

In addition to his certification from Colonel Chang, Mr. Rovere also underwent instructor's training with Major Chang Yen Ying (Chinese Army, retired). Major Chang is a senior student of the legendary martial artist and national hero Do Shen Wu. (Do served at one time as the bodyguard to Dr. Sun Yat Sen.) Major Chang is a former chief instructor of close combat for the Chinese Women's Militia and the "Yu Ge Dwei" (lit. mobile strike teams or commandos) at Changsa and Baoding. As a military unit, the Yu Ge Dwei were specially trained for operations behind enemy lines.

In 1985, Mr. Rovere became the first non-oriental to receive special recognition as a martial artist from the Government of the Republic of China. Additionally, he is the recipient of several other honors including the Chiang Ching Guo (presidential award) for the promotion of Chinese culture overseas.

Mr. Rovere is a qualified expert witness in the areas of physical assault and training methodologies. He is an internationally recognized author, lecturer and security and military training specialist. He holds the distinction of being the only Canadian civilian evaluated and recommended to teach advanced close combat instructor's course to the Canadian military.

In 1995, Mr. Rovere became the first (and currently only) civilian to train in Mainland China with instructors of the Wu Jing (Special Military Police Training Unit), and the Gung An (Public Security). Tasked with training anti-terrorist units, anti-riot teams, and Bo-Biu (bodyguards) for military and government officials, these two training groups represent the best of Chinese military martial arts.

Mr. Rovere currently resides in Calgary, Alberta, Canada where he divides his time between his security consulting and architectural practice, writing, lecturing and conducting seminars.

Interested parties may reach Mr. Rovere through the information presented at the front of the book.